The House of Three

J. Arthur Collins

BookLeaf
Publishing

Presentation by *BookLeaf Publishing*

Web: www.bookleafpub.com

E-mail: info@bookleafpub.com

ISBN: 9789395756976

First edition 2022

DEDICATION

You've read hundreds of books and skimmed this page that same amount.

For once, and for a hundred more henceforth, this page is for you.

My love, my future wife, my light.

Beginning

Welcome to the house of three.
I hope you enjoy your stay
and thrice over you shall see

A minor insight to my pedigree.
On all its walls it will display:
Welcome to the house of three,

A place filled with love and beauty.
Of adoration that lasts ‘till old and gray
And thrice over you shall see

An abode with death in strange delivery
And decay in every hollow hallway.
Welcome to the house of three,

Wherein the walls creak with sounds of me.
The machinations of my thoughts everyday
And thrice over you shall see

Love, death and the inner workings of J. A. C.
Well, shall we go and get things underway?
Welcome to the house of three
And thrice over you shall see.

Want

My sweetest summer servant!
Relent to me your secrets,
Our love far too infrequent.

Please make this day recurrent.
I am without you weakest,
My sweetest summer servant.

You say I'm unobservant,
But I can see your spirits.
Our love far too infrequent.

My father calls a serpent,
But in my bed I'm sleepless.
My sweetest summer servant!

We are quite wealthy merchants,
To you I swear allegiance.
Our love far too infrequent,

Please tell you're just as fervent.
You're in my life's great sequence,
My sweetest summer servant.
Our love far too infrequent.

Withheld

Lift aloft your tether
And dance with the fawns,
To free our love forever.

Pay no mind to weather
And play in the lawns,
Lift aloft your tether.

Give in to this pressure
And sing along sweet songs,
To free our love forever.

Let go of your regressor
And find where heart belongs,
Lift aloft your tether.

Come let us endeavour
And feel how life prolongs,
To free our love forever.

We've no time to dither!
The sun soon comes and dawns.
Lift aloft your tether,
To free our love forever.

Brown

I seek worlds in those brown eyes.
We can travel and explore, please,
Look into mine and let's harmonize.

Allow me, I'll bring the supplies.
Imagine what all we can witness;
I seek worlds in those brown eyes

With cliffs in colour that crystallize
And mountains that only increase.
Look into mine and let's harmonize

And dream of gigantic butterflies,
That drift with us along the breeze.
I seek worlds in those brown eyes,

Through you my own world clarifies.
A land rife with calm and peace,
Look into mine and let's harmonize.

Pure love, your eyes personifies
A world we make our masterpiece.
I seek worlds in those brown eyes;
Look into mine and let's harmonize.

Unique

Oh, some sweet quirks of yours,
I love them all quite much.
I wish to visit all four corners,

In which makes you diverse,
With how one word I blush.
O' some sweet quirks of yours

To go second through doors,
I go huff and you say hush.
I wish to visit all four corners

Of what makes you dangerous,
When in a hurry you must rush.
O' some sweet quirks of yours,

That chocolate is best of all flavours
And it makes your cheeks all flush.
I wish to visit all four corners,

Where is no greater such source,
Of a love when destined to touch.
O' some sweet quirks of yours,
I wish to visit all four corners.

Important

Give unto me, my dear:
Sweet love and emotion,
Your each and every tear.

I wish to feel your fear:
Your bouts of depression.
Give unto me, my dear:

Rays of sunshine's sheer;
Happiness in saturation,
Your each and every tear.

In anger's sore blister,
When mired in contention.
Give unto me, my dear:

Excitement's quite loud clamor.
A feeling with such impression,
Your each and every tear.

I remain, steadfast and bent ear
For every emotional confession.
Give unto me, my dear:
Your each and every tear.

Years

I have but so few years yet to live,
Thus these must be my final pages.
Words upon paper, a gift, to thee: I give.

In letters and stories, aspects of me sure to outlive,
Boundless sources of smiles for my such sweet faces.
I have but so few years yet to live.

A few more of my warblings to put through a sieve.
Locked in my desk: yet more puzzles to take you
ages,
Words upon paper, a gift, to thee: I give.

To be without you, through my heart like a shiv.
Perhaps I'll see you again through one of those cages,
I have but so few years yet to live.

Reincarnation as they say, mayhaps as a cat I'll relive!
My love the same, my body and balance the only
changes,
Words upon paper, a gift, to thee: I give.

O' but silly ramblings from an old man, please
forgive.
You and I such sweet love, through all of life's many
phases.
I have but so few years yet to live,
Words upon paper, a gift, to thee: I give

Humble

I've now seven, with a mere fourteen more.
Not even halfway, you might need some coffee,
I deeply apologize if I am such a bore.

I'm trying everything here with room to explore.
I'd offer you one, but I don't think you want a
copy.
I've now seven, with a mere fourteen more.

You can take a break here for time to restore,
Go take a nap and gain a fresh body.
I deeply apologize if I am such a bore.

It will get better; please, I beg, I implore.
Maybe I got ahead of myself, just a tad too
cocky.
I've now seven, with a mere fourteen more.

I shan't quit my day job, I'll remain in that store;
Was writing twenty-one a literary kamikaze?
I deeply apologize if I am such a bore.

I hope you like poems, there's so much instore:
Sir David Thomas, I'm sure I'll embody.
I've now eight, with a mere thirteen more,
I deeply apologize if I am such a bore.

Transfer

We're comfortable here, it's familiar and warm.
We could become rather used to this:
Spread me your arms, let this be our norm.

The coldest man this warmth could reform;
The toughest man could never resist.
We're comfortable here, it's familiar and warm.

Serenity and rapture, no place for a storm;
Nothing in this moment could go amiss.
Spread me your arms, let this be our norm

In your embrace I feel wholly reborn.
I feel tingly, my legs I'm starting to miss.
We're comfortable here, it's familiar and warm.

Quiet now, slip into the night and conform!
Please relent, this is no longer bliss.
Spread me your arms, let this be our norm.

One remaining thing before you transform!
My lips are the last I feel, I don't wish to kiss.
We're comfortable here, It's familiar and warm,
Spread me your arms, let this be our norm.

Thoughts

Dreams are the mind testing its limits.
A colourful city, a wonderful adventure.
Move one brick and the whole dream pivots.

Time is no matter, with any number of minutes.
The subconscious toying with tedious
conjecture.
Dreams are the mind testing its limits.

To the future to marvel at scientific exhibits.
To the past to experience Einstein's lecture.
Move one brick and the whole dream pivots.

Imagination the only obstacle that inhibits.
Creativity a fickle beast, a necessary creature.
Dreams are the mind testing its limits.

Hold on to your memory as it's only snippets.
Fleeting visions set for a quick departure.
Move one brick and the whole dream pivots.

To relive time with a loved one is worth any
digits.
A momentary manifestation of utter rapture.
Dreams are the mind testing its limits,
Move one brick and the whole dream pivots.

Memory

I worry about forgetfulness.
An unavoidable phenomenon,
And fear for its effects.

Of a fate befit for mindfulness,
An oxymoronic aberration.
I worry about forgetfulness

When I take such carefulness.
Despite the conservation
And fear for its effects.

Of a death of thoughtfulness
And sense of dissolution.
I worry about forgetfulness,

But for some it's quite hopeless.
They will suffer the degradation
And fear for its effects.

I will live a life of happiness
And through deserved consideration,
I worry about forgetfulness
And fear for its effects.

Sticks

There are such times I wish for it's
Sweet release, with utter peace.
Sweet, slow drift through river Styx.

A void as vacant as inert onyx,
Without so much as precious breeze.
There are such times I wish for it's

Stream, a sea devoid of devious politics.
An ocean with no use for prejudice.
Sweet, slow drift through river Styx.

In a world that's choked by epidemics
And ravaged by rampant disease,
There are such times I wish for it's

Currents, coaxing and inviting creaks:
Where all world's life comes to wheeze.
Sweet slow drift through river Styx.

It all sounds okay, take me, my crucifix,
With a mystical presence, a cruel mistress.
There are such times I wish for it's
Sweet, slow drift through river Styx.

Wings

The butterflies are dying
With expedient quickness,
Why did we stop trying?

They're no longer flying
To Mexico with brightness.
The butterflies are dying,

There is no use denying.
This Earth with be lifeless,
Why did we stop trying?

Everyone is vying,
Why, for absolute richness,
The butterflies are dying.

They ignored the warning
And think themselves harmless,
Why did we stop trying?

Our children are crying
And they hear it countless.
The butterflies are dying,
Why did we stop trying?

Close

You nearly got me there.
It was scary and sad,
I wonder if you care

When I faced that scare
And it was all so bad.
You nearly got me there.

In that station of thick air,
From trains built ironclad.
I wonder if you care

That I was on the edge, bare.
Wishing for things I had,
You nearly got me there.

As I took a step fair
And instead, fell and sat.
I wonder if you care

Just how close, I swear.
Are you resentful that
You nearly got me there?
I wonder if you care.

Leaving

Wilting is a worrisome way,
To watch a life be snuffed.
There is no greater dismay:

Than to witness wither midway.
Watch their skin grow rough.
Wilting is a worrisome way,

To see their hair grow gray.
On the floor their final tufts.
There is no greater dismay:

Than to want one more sway,
Of its meticulous graft.
Wilting is a worrisome way,

To feel pages in a fire fray
And soon forget every epigraph.
There is no greater dismay:

Person, pet, plant, book; to pass away;
In our hearts lay their epitaph.
Wilting is a worrisome way.
There is no greater dismay.

Conversation

Oh, another? What shall we use this time?
A Villanelle, I think, she's pretty and
respectable.
Ah, good choice. Such a unique rhyme.

You're getting good at this, but try sublime?
That's not bad, maybe a little expectable.
Oh, another? What shall we use this time?

We need some spice; what about thyme?
A homophone, that's both fun and delectable.
Ah, good choice. Such a unique rhyme.

You know, she's shaping up to be a real dime.
Well, my friend, that's a little objectionable.
Oh, another? What shall we use this time?

I'm stuck on this one, maybe your time to shine?
You just made one, you nonce, truly impeccable.
Ah, good choice. Such a unique rhyme.

Well, that's about it for us. We've hit our prime.
It's been good fun, friends, I hope: unforgettable.
Oh, another? What shall we use this time?
Ah, good choice. Such a unique rhyme.

Ordinary

Wash my bones and comb my brains,
Bake my belly and spoil my eye,
All the things that seem so strange.

Push the cars and pull the trains,
Get run over and never you die,
Wash my bones and comb my brains.

Stand on chairs and walk on canes,
Swim in lava and basements you'll fly,
All the things that seem so strange.

Eat some rope and drink some chains,
Hang off a mountain and rely on a tie,
Wash my bones and comb my brains.

Paint my hair and cross my veins,
Break my elbow and preserve my thigh,
All the things that seem so strange.

Own a house and no complains,
Love a career and enjoy a lie.
Wash my bones and comb my brains,
All the things that seem so strange.

Size

I prefer my poems large
And I like what I prefer,
So let me fight that urge.

You refuse? I'm in charge!
Please kneel and defer.
I prefer my poems large.

Call me the searge.
Hand to head: "yes, sir!"
So let me fight that urge.

Through the door I'll barge,
In and out in a blur.
I prefer my poems large.

My secrets I won't splurge,
In my sleep I do not stir.
So let me fight that urge.

This feeling I shall purge
On the tongue like a slur.
I prefer my poems large,
So let me fight that urge.

English

Grammar is a funny thing; tricky tools for those who care.
One should think it would be so simple:
Letters, words, dots, and numbers; yet so many unaware.

Rules and laws; if you knew them all you'd be a
millionaire.
Simple if not for the umpteenth symbol.
Grammar is a funny thing; tricky tools for those who care.

Centuries spent perfecting, yet most difficult they declare.
If done right it can sound quite hymnal.
Letters, words, dots, and numbers; yet so many unaware

You’re or your,; pick the right one or I'll kill you, I swear.
To dodge my blow you must be nimble.
Grammar is a funny thing; tricky tools for those who care.

Compounds, it all confounds; I before e except for heir.
Acronyms, homonyms, three dashes? — sinful.
Letters, words, dots, and numbers; yet so many unaware.

This language is messy; standout and don't be a square.
Except for high school: then you'll be in a pickle.
Grammar is a funny thing; tricky tools for those who care.
Letters, words, dots, and numbers; yet so many unaware.

Roads

The highway feels designed to steal your senses.
Shake the temptation to deny your creativity.
Take the back roads and smell the efflorescence.

Time to me is of no special essence.
Despite the surrounding, you're not in captivity.
The highway feels designed to steal your senses.

A sea of red, us all creating bioluminescence.
I don't blame you, my neighbours, for your inactivity.
Take the back roads and smell the efflorescence.

The crash culprits sit and watch our coalescence.
Consider, what a time for unexpected productivity.
The highway feels designed to steal your senses.

While we watch the carnage and revert to
adolescence,
But we pass it now and continue along the symmetry.
Take the back roads and smell the efflorescence.

The rush hour ends, goodbye to freeway
incandescence.
I see the exit, a sweet return to the old country.
The highway feels designed to steal your senses,
Take the back roads and smell the efflorescence.

Wishful

O', to be with the greats:
The Edgar Allen Poe's,
A name with such grace.

Poet king of old Thrace,
Orpheus upon his thrones.
O', to be with the greats:

Enheduanna, history dictates,
The first poems from her flows.
A name with such grace:

Mark Twain in his estates,
which he would compose.
O', to be with the greats.

Such beauty she creates:
Gwendolyn Brooks' ordinary woes,
A name with such grace.

My name near their slates,
J. Arthur Collins: I'll superimpose.
O', to be with the greats,
A name with such grace.

CPSIA information can be obtained
at www.ICGtesting.com
Printed in the USA
BVHW050457070723
666786BV00015B/675

9 789395 756976